Hudson

Travel Guide

Your Ultimate Travel Companion for Unforgettable Adventures

Tyler Rivers

Disclaimer

The pictures featured in this book are for artistic purposes only and do not necessarily represent the actual locations referenced in the text. While every effort has been made to ensure the accuracy of the information contained in this guide, neither the author nor the publisher assumes any responsibility for errors or omissions, or for any consequences arising from the use of the information contained herein.

Table of Content

CHAPTER 1

INTRODUCTION TO THE HUDSON VALLEY

Welcome to the Hudson Valley, a captivating and picturesque region located just a stone's throw away from the bustling metropolis of New York City. Nestled between the Catskill Mountains and the Hudson River, this enchanting area is renowned for its natural beauty, rich history, and vibrant cultural scene. Whether you're a nature enthusiast, history buff, art lover, or foodie, the Hudson Valley offers a wealth of experiences that will leave you spellbound.

Overview of the Region

The Hudson Valley spans approximately 150 miles from the northern tip of Manhattan to Albany, the state capital of New York. This diverse and captivating region encompasses a myriad of landscapes, including rolling hills, lush forests, sparkling rivers, and charming towns. Its proximity to New York City has made it a popular getaway for both locals and tourists seeking respite from the urban hustle and bustle.

Geography and Climate

The geography of the Hudson Valley is shaped by the majestic Hudson River, which flows through the heart of the region, serving as a lifeline and a source of inspiration for centuries. The river, flanked by towering cliffs and verdant valleys, offers breathtaking vistas at every turn. In addition to the river, the Hudson Valley is home to countless state parks, nature reserves, and protected areas, providing ample opportunities for outdoor exploration and recreation.

The climate in the Hudson Valley is characterized by four distinct seasons. Summers are warm and pleasant, with temperatures ranging from the 70s to the 90s Fahrenheit (20s to 30s Celsius). Spring and autumn bring mild temperatures and vibrant foliage, painting the landscape in hues of red, orange, and gold. Winters can be chilly, with temperatures often dropping below freezing, transforming the region into a winter wonderland.

History and Cultural Significance

The Hudson Valley boasts a rich historical heritage that dates back centuries. The region played a pivotal role in the early days of European colonization in North America, serving as a gateway to the New World.

It was here, in the Hudson Valley, that Dutch settlers established the colony of New Netherland in the early 17th century, leaving an indelible mark on the region's architecture, traditions, and cultural fabric.

The Hudson Valley also witnessed significant events during the American Revolutionary War, with battles fought on its soil and key figures such as General George Washington making their mark in the region. Today, visitors can explore a plethora of historic sites, including sprawling estates, grand mansions, and meticulously preserved towns that offer a glimpse into the region's storied past.

In addition to its historical significance, the Hudson Valley is a thriving cultural hub. It has been a source of inspiration for generations of artists, writers, and musicians, with its stunning landscapes and serene beauty serving as a muse. The region is home to renowned art galleries, museums, and performance venues, showcasing the creativity and talent that flourishes within its borders.

The culinary scene in the Hudson Valley is equally impressive, with farm-to-table dining, vineyards, and craft breweries offering a delectable array of local flavors and artisanal products.

From fresh produce sourced from local farms to award-winning wines and spirits, the region's gastronomic offerings are a true feast for the senses.

As you embark on your journey through the pages of this Hudson Valley Travel Guide, prepare to be captivated by the region's natural splendor, enchanted by its storied past, and immersed in its vibrant cultural tapestry. Whether you're planning a weekend getaway or an extended exploration, this guide will serve as your trusted companion, providing insider tips, recommended itineraries, and hidden gems that will make your visit to the Hudson Valley an unforgettable experience.

So pack your bags, put on your walking shoes, and get ready to embark on a remarkable adventure through the Hudson Valley. The wonders of this captivating region await you.

CHAPTER 2

GETTING TO THE HUDSON VALLEY

Airports and Transportation Options

The Hudson Valley is conveniently accessible through various airports and transportation options, making it an easy destination to reach from different parts of the country and the world. Whether you prefer to fly or take a scenic road trip, there are multiple ways to get to the Hudson Valley region.

1. Stewart International Airport

One of the major airports serving the Hudson Valley is Stewart International Airport, located in New Windsor, New York. This airport offers domestic and limited international flights, providing a convenient gateway for travelers coming from different parts of the United States. Stewart International Airport is approximately a one-hour drive from New York City, making it an accessible choice for those flying in from other countries.

2. Albany International Airport

Situated in the state capital of New York, Albany International Airport serves as another option for travelers visiting the Hudson Valley. It is located approximately two hours north of New York City.

Albany International Airport offers a range of domestic flights and connects the region to various major cities across the United States.

3. Westchester County Airport

For those looking to explore the southern part of the Hudson Valley, Westchester County Airport is a convenient choice. Located in White Plains, New York, this airport offers domestic flights and is situated just 33 miles north of Manhattan. It serves as a gateway to the lower Hudson Valley region, providing easy access to popular destinations such as Tarrytown, Sleepy Hollow, and Yonkers.

4. New York City Airports

Travelers can also consider flying into one of the major airports in New York City, such as John F. Kennedy International Airport (JFK) or LaGuardia Airport (LGA). These airports offer a wide range of domestic and international flights and are well-connected to the Hudson Valley region through various transportation options, including trains, buses, and car rentals.

Car Rental and Road Networks

Renting a car is an excellent option for exploring the Hudson Valley at your own pace and experiencing its scenic beauty. Several car rental agencies operate in the area, offering a variety of vehicles to suit different needs.

The Hudson Valley is well-connected by a network of highways, making it easily accessible by road. The region is primarily served by Interstate 87 (I-87), also known as the New York State Thruway, which runs north-south through the Hudson Valley. This major highway provides convenient access to various cities and towns in the region.

Additionally, there are several other highways and scenic byways that crisscross the Hudson Valley, offering picturesque routes and opportunities to explore charming towns along the way. Some notable routes include Route 9, Route 9W, and the Taconic State Parkway.

Public Transportation and Train Services

For those who prefer public transportation, the Hudson Valley offers several options, including train services and buses.

Metro-North Railroad operates train services that connect the Hudson Valley to New York City. The Hudson Line, specifically, runs along the eastern bank of the Hudson River, offering scenic views of the water and the surrounding landscapes. The train stops at various towns and cities in the region, including Poughkeepsie, Beacon, Cold Spring, and Croton-Harmon.

Amtrak also provides train services to the Hudson Valley, with stops in cities like Albany, Poughkeepsie, and Rhinecliff. These services connect the region to other major cities on the East Coast, making it convenient for travelers coming from farther away.

In addition to train services, several bus companies operate in the Hudson Valley, offering transportation within the region and connections to neighboring areas. These buses provide an affordable alternative for travelers who prefer not to drive or fly.

Whether you choose to fly, drive, or take public transportation, the Hudson Valley offers multiple options to reach the region comfortably. With its well-connected airports, road networks, and train services, getting to the Hudson Valley is a breeze, allowing you to begin your adventure and explore all that this picturesque region has to offer.

CHAPTER 3

EXPLORING THE HUDSON VALLEY

The Hudson Valley is a region brimming with captivating cities, picturesque towns, breathtaking natural beauty, and a rich historical and cultural heritage. In this chapter, we will delve into the various facets of the Hudson Valley, guiding you through its major cities and towns, exploring its natural attractions and parks, uncovering its historic sites and landmarks, and immersing ourselves in its vibrant cultural and arts scene.

Major Cities and Towns

The Hudson Valley is home to several noteworthy cities and towns, each with its unique character and charm. Let's take a closer look at some of the region's prominent destinations.

1. Albany

Situated at the northern end of the Hudson Valley, Albany, the capital of New York State, offers a blend of rich history and modern amenities. Explore the New York State Capitol, an architectural marvel, and visit the Albany Institute of History and Art, which houses an impressive collection of artwork and artifacts.

Take a stroll through the vibrant downtown area, where you'll find an array of restaurants, shops, and entertainment venues.

2. Poughkeepsie

Located on the eastern bank of the Hudson River, Poughkeepsie is known for its stunning waterfront, historic sites, and lively atmosphere. Cross the Mid-Hudson Bridge for breathtaking views of the river and visit the Walkway Over the Hudson, the longest elevated pedestrian bridge in the world. Explore the charming streets of the city's downtown area, lined with eclectic shops, cozy cafes, and delightful restaurants.

3. Kingston

As the first capital of New York State, Kingston is steeped in history and offers a glimpse into the region's colonial past. Discover the Historic Stockade District, a neighborhood adorned with well-preserved 17th-century stone houses. Visit the Senate House State Historic Site, where the first New York State Senate convened. Enjoy the city's vibrant arts scene, with numerous galleries showcasing local talent.

4. Newburgh

Situated on the western banks of the Hudson River, Newburgh boasts a rich maritime history and stunning river views. Take a stroll along the waterfront promenade and visit the historic Ritz Theater, which hosts a variety of live performances. Explore Washington's Headquarters State Historic Site, where General George Washington set up his command during the Revolutionary War. Don't miss the opportunity to take a scenic boat tour along the Hudson River.

Natural Attractions and Parks

The Hudson Valley is blessed with an abundance of natural beauty, from rolling hills to majestic mountains and picturesque river valleys. Let's explore some of the region's most notable natural attractions and parks.

1. Bear Mountain State Park

Nestled in the rugged terrain of the Hudson Highlands, Bear Mountain State Park offers breathtaking vistas, miles of hiking trails, and recreational activities for outdoor enthusiasts. Climb to the summit of Bear Mountain and savor panoramic views of the Hudson River and surrounding landscapes. Explore the zoo, picnic by the lake, or paddle a kayak on Hessian Lake.

2. Catskill Park

Encompassing over 700,000 acres of pristine wilderness, Catskill Park is a haven for nature lovers. Discover cascading waterfalls, meandering streams, and verdant forests as you explore the park's extensive trail network. Visit Kaaterskill Falls, one of the tallest waterfalls in New York State, and hike to the fire tower on Hunter Mountain for breathtaking panoramic views.

3. Minnewaska State Park Preserve

Located on the Shawangunk Mountain ridge, Minnewaska State Park Preserve offers a tranquil escape amidst stunning natural beauty. Hike along the park's well-maintained trails, marvel at the pristine glacial lakes, and enjoy scenic overlooks with sweeping views of the surrounding valleys. Take a refreshing dip in Lake Minnewaska or explore the fascinating rock formations and caves.

4. Storm King Art Center

Combining art with nature, the Storm King Art Center is a unique outdoor museum set on 500 acres of rolling hills, fields, and woodlands. Discover a collection of over 100 sculptures created by renowned artists, including Alexander Calder and Mark di Suvero.

Wander along the trails, interact with the artwork, and experience the harmonious blend of art and nature.

Historic Sites and Landmarks

The Hudson Valley is steeped in history, with numerous historic sites and landmarks that offer a glimpse into the region's past. Let's explore some of these captivating destinations.

1. Franklin D. Roosevelt National Historic Site

Step back in time at the Franklin D. Roosevelt National Historic Site in Hyde Park. Visit Springwood, the beloved home of President Franklin D. Roosevelt, and explore the Presidential Library and Museum, which houses an extensive collection of artifacts and exhibits chronicling FDR's presidency and the Great Depression.

2. West Point Military Academy

Located on the west bank of the Hudson River, the United States Military Academy at West Point is a revered institution with a rich military heritage. Take a guided tour of the campus, visit the West Point Museum, and witness the precision and discipline of the cadets during a military parade.

3. Olana State Historic Site

Perched atop a hill overlooking the Hudson River, Olana State Historic Site is the former home of renowned Hudson River School painter Frederic Edwin Church. Explore the Persian-inspired mansion, stroll through the meticulously landscaped gardens, and soak in the panoramic views that inspired Church's masterpieces.

4. Vanderbilt Mansion National Historic Site

Transport yourself to the Gilded Age at the Vanderbilt Mansion National Historic Site in Hyde Park. Marvel at the grandeur of the Vanderbilt Mansion, a magnificent Beaux-Arts mansion set amidst beautifully landscaped gardens. Learn about the Vanderbilt family's lavish lifestyle and the social history of the era.

Cultural and Arts Scene

The Hudson Valley has long been a haven for artists, musicians, and performers, offering a vibrant cultural scene. Let's explore some of the region's cultural and arts destinations.

1. Dia:Beacon

Located in Beacon, Dia:Beacon is a renowned contemporary art museum housed in a former Nabisco box-printing factory. Explore the vast exhibition spaces, which showcase thought-provoking installations and large-scale artworks. Experience the fusion of art and architecture in this unique gallery.

2. Woodstock Art Colony

Immerse yourself in the artistic legacy of the Woodstock Art Colony in Woodstock. Visit the Woodstock Artists Association & Museum, which preserves and showcases the work of local artists. Explore the town's art galleries, attend art festivals, and witness the creative energy that continues to thrive in this renowned artist community.

3. Bardavon Opera House

Located in Poughkeepsie, the Bardavon Opera House is a historic theater that hosts a wide range of performances, including music concerts, Broadway shows, and dance performances. Take in a live show in this beautifully restored venue, which dates back to 1869, and experience the magic of the performing arts.

As you explore the Hudson Valley, you'll discover a region that seamlessly blends natural beauty, historical significance, and artistic expression. Whether you're hiking along scenic trails, immersing yourself in the region's rich history, or enjoying a performance in one of its vibrant arts venues, the Hudson Valley offers a diverse array of experiences that will leave you captivated and inspired.

CHAPTER 4

OUTDOOR ACTIVITIES IN THE HUDSON VALLEY

The Hudson Valley is not only known for its stunning landscapes and historical sites but also for its abundance of outdoor activities that cater to nature enthusiasts and adventure seekers alike. Whether you enjoy hiking through lush forests, kayaking along scenic rivers, or hitting the slopes during the winter months, this region offers a wide range of opportunities to connect with nature and indulge in thrilling outdoor pursuits.

Hiking and Biking Trails

The Hudson Valley boasts an extensive network of hiking and biking trails, making it a haven for outdoor enthusiasts who love to explore on foot or two wheels. From beginner-friendly paths to more challenging routes, there is something for everyone to enjoy.

One popular hiking destination is Bear Mountain State Park, located on the west bank of the Hudson River. The park offers a variety of well-marked trails that wind through dense woodlands, offering breathtaking views of the surrounding valleys and the Hudson River. The Appalachian Trail, one of the most famous long-distance hiking trails in the United States, passes through this park, attracting hikers from far and wide.

For those who prefer biking, the Dutchess Rail Trail provides a scenic and tranquil experience. This 13-mile trail follows the former Maybrook Rail Line and takes cyclists through picturesque towns, rolling farmland, and over charming bridges. With its gentle gradients and well-maintained surface, the Dutchess Rail Trail is suitable for riders of all skill levels.

Water Activities

The Hudson Valley's numerous rivers, lakes, and reservoirs offer ample opportunities for water-based activities. Kayaking and canoeing are popular choices for those seeking a serene and immersive experience on the water.

One notable waterway is the Hudson River itself, which stretches for approximately 315 miles and provides an array of paddling possibilities. Adventurous kayakers can explore the river's diverse ecosystems, encountering breathtaking scenery and a rich variety of wildlife along the way.

Several outfitters in the region offer guided tours and kayak rentals, ensuring a safe and enjoyable experience for both beginners and experienced paddlers.

Sailing and boating enthusiasts will also find plenty to indulge in within the Hudson Valley. The river's wide expanse and gentle currents make it an ideal location for leisurely cruises and sailing adventures. Whether you choose to bring your own vessel or rent one from a local marina, navigating the Hudson River offers a unique perspective on the surrounding landscape and historic sites.

Fishing is another popular activity in the Hudson Valley, with its abundant waterways teeming with various fish species. Anglers can cast their lines in rivers, lakes, and reservoirs, hoping to reel in trout, bass, perch, and more. Fishing charters and guides are available for those seeking expert assistance or local insights into the best fishing spots and techniques.

Golf Courses and Country Clubs

If you're a golf enthusiast, the Hudson Valley won't disappoint. The region boasts several exceptional golf courses and country clubs that cater to players of all skill levels.

From beautifully manicured fairways to challenging holes nestled within the scenic landscapes, golfers can enjoy a memorable experience while surrounded by the natural beauty of the Hudson Valley.

The Garrison Golf Club, located in Garrison, offers breathtaking views of the Hudson River and the surrounding hills. This challenging 18-hole course, designed by Dick Wilson, features undulating fairways, strategically placed bunkers, and stunning water hazards. Golfers can test their skills while soaking in the serene ambiance of this picturesque setting.

For those seeking a more relaxed golfing experience, the Mohonk Mountain House Golf Course provides a unique opportunity to play amidst the Shawangunk Mountains. This 9-hole course offers breathtaking panoramic views and a peaceful atmosphere. After a round of golf, players can unwind at the historic Mohonk Mountain House, a grand Victorian castle resort.

Winter Sports and Ski Resorts

When winter blankets the Hudson Valley with snow, it transforms into a winter wonderland, offering a host of exhilarating outdoor activities.

Ski resorts in the region attract snow enthusiasts from near and far, providing opportunities for skiing, snowboarding, and other winter sports.

Hunter Mountain, located in the Catskill Mountains, is one of the premier ski destinations in the Hudson Valley. With its diverse terrain, the mountain offers trails suitable for beginners as well as challenging runs for experienced skiers and snowboarders. State-of-the-art facilities, equipment rentals, and professional instructors ensure a safe and enjoyable experience for visitors of all skill levels.

Windham Mountain Resort, also situated in the Catskills, is another popular winter sports destination. With its well-groomed trails, a variety of terrain parks, and family-friendly atmosphere, Windham Mountain caters to skiers, snowboarders, and winter sports enthusiasts of all ages.

For those who prefer a more tranquil winter experience, cross-country skiing and snowshoeing are excellent options to explore the snowy landscapes of the Hudson Valley. Many parks and nature preserves, such as Minnewaska State Park Preserve and Fahnestock Winter Park, offer designated trails for these activities.

Whether you prefer hiking, biking, water activities, golfing, or winter sports, the Hudson Valley provides an abundance of outdoor activities to suit every interest and skill level. From serene nature walks to adrenaline-pumping adventures, this region offers a remarkable range of experiences for outdoor enthusiasts, ensuring that your time spent in the Hudson Valley is unforgettable.

CHAPTER 5

FOOD AND DRINK IN THE HUDSON VALLEY

The Hudson Valley is not only a haven for natural beauty and historical landmarks, but it also boasts a vibrant food and drink scene that tantalizes the taste buds of locals and visitors alike. With its fertile farmlands, thriving culinary communities, and a commitment to farm-to-table dining, the region offers a delectable array of flavors and experiences. In this chapter, we will explore the culinary delights and libations that make the Hudson Valley a true gastronomic destination.

Farm-to-Table Dining

One of the defining characteristics of the Hudson Valley's food culture is its emphasis on farm-to-table dining. Restaurants throughout the region prioritize sourcing their ingredients locally, often from nearby farms and producers. This commitment to using fresh, seasonal, and locally-sourced ingredients ensures that every meal is a celebration of the region's agricultural bounty.

Imagine savoring a dish made with plump, heirloom tomatoes picked that morning, accompanied by artisanal cheese crafted by a local dairy farm. Or perhaps you'd prefer a tender, grass-fed steak sourced from a nearby ranch, cooked to perfection and served with vegetables harvested from a neighboring farm. The possibilities are endless, and the chefs in the Hudson Valley take pride in showcasing the flavors of the region through their culinary creations.

Wineries and Vineyards

The Hudson Valley is home to a flourishing wine industry, with vineyards and wineries dotting the picturesque landscapes. From rolling hillsides to riverside estates, the region's wineries offer a diverse selection of wines that are sure to please even the most discerning oenophile.

Take a leisurely stroll through the vineyards, learn about the winemaking process, and indulge in tastings that showcase the unique terroir of the Hudson Valley. From crisp and refreshing whites to robust reds, the wines of the region reflect the care and dedication of the winemakers who have embraced the Hudson Valley's potential as a premier wine destination.

Craft Breweries and Distilleries

In addition to its wineries, the Hudson Valley is also gaining recognition for its craft breweries and distilleries. These establishments pride themselves on producing high-quality beers, ales, and spirits using traditional methods and locally-sourced ingredients. Whether you're a beer enthusiast or a whiskey connoisseur, you'll find a wide range of flavors and styles to explore.

Visit a local brewery to witness the brewing process firsthand, or stop by a distillery to learn about the art of distillation and sample their unique creations. From hoppy IPAs to rich stouts, and from small-batch bourbons to artisanal gins, the Hudson Valley's craft beverages offer a delightful sensory journey that highlights the region's commitment to craftsmanship and innovation.

Farmers Markets and Culinary Experiences

To truly immerse yourself in the Hudson Valley's food culture, a visit to one of its farmers markets is a must. These vibrant marketplaces are brimming with fresh produce, artisanal products, and homemade treats. Stroll through the stalls, chat with local farmers and artisans, and discover an array of ingredients that will inspire your own culinary adventures.

Many farmers markets also offer cooking demonstrations, where talented chefs showcase their skills and provide insights into preparing dishes with the season's best ingredients. It's an opportunity to learn new techniques, gather recipe ideas, and engage with the culinary community of the Hudson Valley.

For those seeking more immersive experiences, the region offers culinary tours, workshops, and farm visits. Join a guided tour that takes you behind the scenes of a local cheese-making operation or spend a day on a farm, participating in hands-on activities such as harvesting vegetables or feeding livestock. These experiences provide a deeper understanding of the region's food production and allow you to connect with the people who are at the heart of the Hudson Valley's culinary renaissance.

The Hudson Valley's food and drink scene is a testament to the region's rich agricultural heritage and the passion of its culinary community. From farm-to-table restaurants to vineyards, craft breweries, and farmers markets, every bite and sip in the Hudson Valley tells a story of tradition, innovation, and a deep connection to the land. Embark on a gastronomic journey through the Hudson Valley and savor the flavors that make this region a true epicurean paradise.

CHAPTER 6

SHOPPING AND ENTERTAINMENT

The Hudson Valley is not only known for its stunning natural beauty and rich history but also for its vibrant shopping and entertainment scene. Whether you're a shopaholic, an art enthusiast, or a lover of live performances, the region offers a plethora of options to cater to every taste. In this chapter, we will explore the diverse shopping opportunities, art galleries, performing arts venues, and exciting festivals and events that make the Hudson Valley a true cultural haven.

Shopping Delights

The Hudson Valley is a paradise for those seeking unique shopping experiences. From charming boutiques to expansive outlet malls, the region has something for everyone. Let's embark on a journey through some of the top shopping destinations in the Hudson Valley:

1. Boutique Treasures

The small towns and villages of the Hudson Valley are dotted with delightful boutiques offering an array of one-of-a-kind items. In Rhinebeck, you'll find quaint shops that showcase handmade crafts, vintage clothing, and eclectic home decor.

Hudson, with its vibrant arts community, boasts stylish boutiques selling contemporary fashion, artisanal jewelry, and modern home furnishings. And in Woodstock, explore the bohemian boutiques filled with hippie-chic clothing, unique accessories, and holistic wellness products.

2. Outlet Shopping

For those seeking great deals and designer brands, the Hudson Valley's outlet malls are a shopper's paradise. The Woodbury Common Premium Outlets, located in Central Valley, features over 250 high-end designer stores offering discounts on clothing, accessories, and home goods. The Poughkeepsie Galleria Mall is another popular shopping destination, featuring a wide range of retailers, from department stores to specialty shops.

3. Farmers Markets and Artisanal Products

Indulge in the farm-to-table culture of the Hudson Valley by exploring the numerous farmers markets scattered across the region. From fresh produce and organic meats to handcrafted cheeses and artisanal chocolates, these markets offer a feast for the senses. The Rhinebeck Farmers Market, located in the heart of the village, is a must-visit for its wide selection of local goods and lively atmosphere.

Art Galleries and Cultural Experiences

The Hudson Valley has long been a haven for artists and art enthusiasts. The region is home to a thriving arts scene, with numerous galleries showcasing a diverse range of artistic styles and mediums. Here are a few noteworthy art galleries in the area:

1. Dia:Beacon

Located in Beacon, Dia:Beacon is a renowned contemporary art museum housed in a former Nabisco box-printing factory. This expansive gallery space showcases large-scale installations and exhibits by internationally acclaimed artists. Spend a day immersed in the thought-provoking and visually stunning works that grace the museum's halls.

2. Storm King Art Center

Situated in New Windsor, the Storm King Art Center is an outdoor sculpture park spanning over 500 acres of rolling hills, fields, and woodlands. Wander through the landscape and encounter monumental sculptures by artists such as Alexander Calder, Mark di Suvero, and Maya Lin. The combination of art and nature in this open-air museum is a truly immersive experience.

3. Woodstock Art Colony

Immerse yourself in the artistic heritage of the Woodstock Art Colony, which has been a haven for artists since the early 20th century. Explore the galleries and studios that showcase works by local artists inspired by the region's natural beauty. The Woodstock Artists Association and Museum is a must-visit, offering exhibitions that celebrate the area's rich artistic legacy.

Performing Arts and Entertainment

The Hudson Valley boasts a vibrant performing arts scene, with theaters, music venues, and cultural events that cater to a wide range of interests. Here are a few highlights:

1. Bardavon Opera House

Located in Poughkeepsie, the Bardavon Opera House is a historic theater that hosts a diverse array of performances, including Broadway shows, musical concerts, dance performances, and film screenings. Immerse yourself in the grandeur of this beautifully restored venue while enjoying world-class entertainment.

2. Bethel Woods Center for the Arts

Situated at the site of the iconic 1969 Woodstock Festival, the Bethel Woods Center for the Arts in Bethel offers a unique cultural experience. Attend concerts by renowned musicians, explore the Woodstock museum, and enjoy outdoor events set against the backdrop of the beautiful Catskill Mountains.

3. Festivals and Events

The Hudson Valley is known for its vibrant festivals and events throughout the year. From music festivals and craft fairs to food and wine events, there's always something happening in the region. The Hudson Valley Garlic Festival in Saugerties, the Clearwater Festival in Croton-on-Hudson, and the Woodstock Film Festival are just a few examples of the diverse and lively events that showcase the region's culture and community spirit.

As you explore the shopping and entertainment offerings in the Hudson Valley, you'll discover a region brimming with creativity, artistic expression, and cultural diversity. Whether you're strolling through charming boutiques, admiring world-class artworks, or immersing yourself in live performances, the Hudson Valley is sure to captivate and inspire you at every turn.

CHAPTER 7

ACCOMMODATIONS IN THE HUDSON VALLEY

When planning your visit to the beautiful Hudson Valley, it's important to consider where you'll be staying during your trip. The region offers a wide range of accommodations to suit every traveler's needs, from luxurious resorts to cozy bed and breakfasts, and everything in between. In this chapter, we will explore the various options available to you and provide recommendations to help you make the most of your stay.

Hotels and Resorts

If you prefer the convenience and amenities of a hotel or resort, the Hudson Valley won't disappoint. From upscale establishments to charming boutique hotels, you'll find a range of options to suit your preferences. Many of these accommodations are located in picturesque settings, offering stunning views of the region's natural beauty.

One highly recommended hotel is the Hudson Valley Grand Resort, nestled amidst the scenic Catskill Mountains. This sprawling resort boasts comfortable rooms, an outdoor pool, a spa, and multiple dining options. Its proximity to popular attractions like Hunter Mountain and Kaaterskill Falls makes it an ideal choice for outdoor enthusiasts.

For those seeking a more historic and elegant experience, The Beekman Arms & Delamater Inn in Rhinebeck is a charming choice. Established in 1766, it is one of the oldest operating inns in America. With its cozy rooms, period furnishings, and a renowned on-site restaurant, it offers a unique blend of old-world charm and modern comfort.

Bed and Breakfasts

For a more intimate and personalized experience, consider staying at one of the many delightful bed and breakfasts scattered throughout the Hudson Valley. These establishments often provide a warm and inviting atmosphere, along with homemade breakfasts that showcase local flavors and ingredients.

The Caldwell House Bed and Breakfast in Salisbury Mills is a hidden gem worth considering. This beautifully restored colonial inn offers elegantly appointed rooms, a delicious breakfast served in a sunlit dining room, and easy access to nearby hiking trails and wineries. The friendly hosts are also happy to provide recommendations for local attractions and dining options.

Another noteworthy option is the Hilltop House Bed and Breakfast in Amenia.

This charming Victorian-era house offers cozy rooms, a lovely garden, and breathtaking views of the surrounding countryside. Guests can savor a homemade breakfast featuring fresh produce from the property's own gardens, ensuring a truly farm-to-table experience.

Vacation Rentals and Cabins

If you're looking for a more independent and secluded experience, renting a vacation home or cabin in the Hudson Valley might be the perfect choice. These accommodations provide privacy and flexibility, allowing you to create your own itinerary and immerse yourself in the region's natural beauty.

The Hudson Valley is dotted with numerous vacation rentals, ranging from cozy cabins nestled in the woods to spacious country estates. Websites like Airbnb and VRBO offer a wide selection of options to suit different group sizes and budgets. Whether you're seeking a romantic retreat for two or a family-friendly getaway, you're sure to find the perfect rental that meets your needs.

Campgrounds and RV Parks

For nature enthusiasts and outdoor adventurers, camping in the Hudson Valley offers an immersive experience surrounded by the region's stunning landscapes. There are several well-equipped campgrounds and RV parks throughout the area, providing facilities and amenities for a comfortable stay.

One popular campground is Kenneth L. Wilson Campground near Woodstock. Nestled in the Catskill Mountains, this picturesque campground offers spacious campsites, picnic areas, and access to hiking trails. With its serene atmosphere and proximity to natural attractions, it's an excellent choice for those seeking a true outdoor getaway.

If you prefer RV camping, Black Bear Campground in Florida, New York, is a top pick. This family-friendly campground features full hook-up sites, clean facilities, and recreational amenities such as a swimming pool and playground. Its convenient location, just a short drive from popular Hudson Valley attractions, makes it a great base for exploring the region.

When it comes to accommodations in the Hudson Valley, you'll find a diverse array of options that cater to different tastes and preferences.

Whether you prefer the luxury of a hotel, the charm of a bed and breakfast, the privacy of a vacation rental, or the outdoor experience of camping, the region has something for everyone. Take the time to consider your needs and interests, and choose the accommodation that will make your visit to the Hudson Valley truly unforgettable.

CHAPTER 8

PRACTICAL INFORMATION

As you embark on your Hudson Valley adventure, it's essential to equip yourself with practical information to ensure a smooth and enjoyable journey. This chapter provides valuable details about visitor centers, safety tips, traveling with pets, and understanding local customs. By familiarizing yourself with this information, you'll be well-prepared to navigate the region and make the most of your visit.

Visitor Centers and Tourist Information

The Hudson Valley is home to several visitor centers and tourist information offices that serve as valuable resources for travelers. These centers are staffed with knowledgeable individuals who can provide maps, brochures, and expert advice on the best places to visit, dine, and stay. They can also assist with booking tours and arranging transportation.

When you arrive in the Hudson Valley, consider stopping by one of the following visitor centers:

1. **Hudson Valley Tourism**: Located in the heart of the region, this comprehensive tourist information center offers a wealth of resources and insider tips. They can

provide you with detailed itineraries, information about upcoming events, and recommendations tailored to your interests.

2. **Regional Tourism Offices**: Each county in the Hudson Valley has its own tourism office, staffed with local experts who possess in-depth knowledge about their specific area. These offices can provide you with specific information about attractions, accommodations, and dining options in their respective counties.

3. **National Park Service Visitor Centers**: If you plan to explore the region's national parks, such as the Franklin D. Roosevelt National Historic Site or the Vanderbilt Mansion National Historic Site, be sure to visit their visitor centers. Here, you can learn about the park's history, pick up trail maps, and gather insights from park rangers.

Remember, visitor centers are there to enhance your experience and answer any questions you may have. Don't hesitate to seek their guidance as you plan your Hudson Valley journey.

Safety Tips and Emergency Contacts

While the Hudson Valley is generally a safe destination, it's always wise to take certain precautions to ensure your well-being. Here are some safety tips to keep in mind during your visit:

1. Stay Informed: Familiarize yourself with the local weather forecast and any potential hazards or advisories. It's important to be aware of any changes that could impact your travel plans.

2. Be Prepared for Outdoor Activities: If you plan to engage in outdoor activities like hiking or boating, make sure to bring appropriate gear, including sturdy footwear, insect repellent, sunscreen, and ample water. Follow trail markers and safety guidelines to avoid any mishaps.

3. Secure Your Belongings: Keep your valuables secure while exploring the Hudson Valley. Avoid leaving belongings unattended in public spaces and consider using hotel safes or locking your car when necessary.

4. Follow Traffic Laws: When driving through the Hudson Valley, adhere to speed limits, wear seat belts, and avoid distractions. Familiarize yourself with parking regulations in each area to avoid fines.

In case of emergencies, it's crucial to have access to local emergency contacts. Make a note of the following numbers:

- Police, Fire, and Medical Emergencies: Dial 911

- Hudson Valley Regional Poison Control Center: [Insert local poison control center number]

Remember, your safety is paramount, and by following these tips, you can enjoy a worry-free experience in the Hudson Valley.

Traveling with Pets

For those traveling with furry companions, the Hudson Valley welcomes pets in many outdoor areas, but it's essential to be mindful of local rules and etiquette. Here are some guidelines to ensure a pet-friendly experience:

1. Research Pet-Friendly Attractions: Before setting out on your adventure, research attractions, parks, and trails that allow pets. Some places may have specific leash requirements or restricted areas, so familiarize yourself with these details in advance.

2. Bring the Essentials: Pack essentials for your pet, including food, water, a leash, waste bags, and any

necessary medications. Consider bringing a pet first aid kit for any unexpected situations.

3. Respect Others: While exploring public spaces, ensure your pet is well-behaved and doesn't disturb other visitors. Always clean up after your pet and dispose of waste responsibly.

4. Accommodation Considerations: When booking accommodations, confirm that they are pet-friendly and inquire about any additional fees or restrictions. Some hotels may have designated pet-friendly rooms or areas.

By adhering to these guidelines, you and your furry companion can enjoy the beauty of the Hudson Valley together.

Useful Phrases and Local Customs

Immersing yourself in the local culture can greatly enhance your experience in the Hudson Valley. Here are some useful phrases and insights into local customs that will help you connect with the residents and navigate the region:

1. **Greetings**: When meeting someone, a simple "Hello" or "Hi" is appropriate. Handshakes are the customary form of greeting in formal settings.

2. **Politeness**: The people of the Hudson Valley value politeness and courteous behavior. Saying "Please" and "Thank you" goes a long way in establishing positive interactions.

3. **Tipping**: Tipping is customary in the United States, including the Hudson Valley. In restaurants, it is customary to tip around 15-20% of the total bill. Tipping is also common for services such as taxis, tour guides, and hotel staff.

4. **Cultural Sensitivity**: Respect the diversity and cultural heritage of the Hudson Valley. Be mindful of appropriate attire when visiting religious or sacred sites and show reverence in these spaces.

5. **Engage in Conversation**: The residents of the Hudson Valley are known for their friendliness. Strike up conversations with locals, ask for recommendations, and show an interest in their community.

By embracing the local customs and engaging with the people of the Hudson Valley, you'll create lasting memories and build connections that enrich your travel experience.

Printed by Amazon Italia Logistica S.r.l.
Torrazza Piemonte (TO), Italy

59960762R00030